AF527578

THE INDIAN CONTRACT ACT, 1987

1st Edition

(Part-1)

Ms. Honey Thakkar

Research Scholar & Assistant Professor

ISBN NO. 978-93-6012-864-7

THAKKAR GOVINDBHAI PRABHUDAS

Dedicated to my beloved father
There will always be a few people who
have the courage to love what is untamed inside us.
One of those men is my father.

Acknowledgment

I am deeply grateful for the opportunity to write and publish this book, as it has been a lifelong dream of mine. I would like to express my sincere gratitude to everyone who has supported me throughout this journey.

First and foremost, I would like to thank my mom, dad, brother and my friends for their unwavering love, encouragement, and believe in my potential and abilities. Their constant support and understanding have been instrumental in making this book a reality.

I extend my heartfelt to my mentor, [Dr. Parima Raval], whose guidance and expertise have been instrumental in honing my writing skills. Their commitment to excellence and dedication to my growth as an author have been truly inspiring..

Lastly, I want to acknowledge the readers of this book. Your interest and support means the world to me. It is my sincere hope that this book will resonate with you and provide insights, inspiration, and interesting explanatory pictures.

To all those who have played a major part, in Creating this self explanatory book that even a layman can understand the concept of contract easily, I am thankful from the bottom of my heart. Your valuable contributions have made this dream come true, and I am eternally grateful.

With my deep gratitude,
[Honey Govindbhai Thakkar]
Research Scholar & Assistant Professor

Table of Contents:

The Indian Contract Act, 1872: An overview of Sections 1 to 75 covering the general nature of contract, consideration, other essential elements of a valid contract, performance of contract, breach of contract, Contingent and Quasi Contract

CHAPTER VI
OF THE CONSEQUENCES OF BREACH OF CONTRACT

THE INDIAN CONTRACT ACT, 1872

➢ **Introduction –**

1. **INDIAN CONTRACT ACT, 1872** governs law relating to contracts in India.
2. The Act was **passed by British India** and is based on the principles of English Common Law.
3. This Act is applicable to **whole of India including Jammu and Kashmir**.
4. The Act came into effect **from 1st September, 1872** and applies to all contracts in India.

➢ Important Definitions under the Act –

1) **Proposal – Sec 2(a)**
When one person signifies to another his willingness to do or to abstain from doing anything, with a view to obtaining the assent of that other to such act or abstinence, he is said to make a proposal.

2) **Acceptance – Sec 2(b)**
When the person to whom the proposal is made signifies his assent thereto, the proposal is said to be accepted. **A proposal, when accepted, becomes a promise**
Person making the proposal is called the "**promisor**", and the person accepting the proposal is called the "**promisee**".

3) **Agreement – Sec 2(e)**

Every promise and every set of promises, forming the consideration for each other, is an agreement.
In simple words, Agreement = Offer + Acceptance

4) **Void Agreement – Sec 2(g)**

An agreement not enforceable by law is said to be void.

5) **Contract – Sec 2(h)**

An agreement enforceable by law is called as contract. In simple words, Contract = Agreement + Enforceability.

6) **Voidable Contract –**

An agreement which is enforceable by law at the option of one or more of the parties thereto, but not at the option of the other or others.

➢ Is every agreement contract?

1) **No,** every agreement is not a contract.
2) An agreement to become a contract must give rise to a **legal obligation (duty)**
3) **An agreement can be –**

Social Obligation

- An agreement giving rise to social obligation is not a contract
- Not covered under ICA, 1872 (Indian Contract Act, 1872)

Legal Obligation

- Agreement giving rise to legal obligation is a contract
- Covered under ICA, 1872

Example ⇩

a) An agreement between two persons to go together to the cinema, or for a walk, or for a dinner is an agreement of social nature and not covered under Indian Contract Act, 1872.
b) Domestic agreement between husband and wife is also not a contract.

Every contract is an agreement, but every agreement is not a contract

➢ **Difference Between Agreement and Contract –**

BASIS FOR COMPARISO N	AGREEMENT	CONTRACT
Meaning	When a proposal is accepted by the person to whom it is made, with requisite consideration, it is an agreement.	When an agreement is enforceable by law, it becomes a contract.

Elements	Offer and Acceptance	Agreement and Enforceability
Defined in	Section 2 (e)	Section 2 (h)
In writing	Not necessarily	Normally written and registered
Legal obligation	Does not creates legal obligation	Creates legal obligation
One in other	Every agreement need not be a contract.	All contracts are agreement
Scope	Wide	Narrow

➤ Essential elements of a valid contract –

Under Section 10 –	Not given under section 10 but still are essentials of valid contract –
a) Agreement b) Free Consent c) Competency of the parties d) Lawful Consideration e) Legal object f) Not expressly declared to be void	a) Two parties b) Intention to create legal relationship c) Legal formalities d) Certainty of meaning e) Possibility of performance

1) **Two parties –**There should be at least 2 parties for a contract.

2) **Offer –** There shall be an offer or proposal by one party.

3) **Acceptance –** Offer made should be accepted by the other party

4) **Lawful consideration –** The agreement shall be supported by lawful consideration

5) **Lawful object –** The object and consideration of the contract shall be legal

6) **Competent (capacity) to contract – Section 11**
   a) The parties to the contract shall be competent to contract

b) For a person to become competent to contract –
   - Such person should be major (18+)
   - Such person should be of sound mind (Section 12)
   - Such person should not be disqualified by law

7) Free consent –

a) There shall be free consent between the parties to the contract
b) Consent is said to be free when the following elements are absent (Section 14)
   - Coercion (Section 15)
   - Undue influence (Section 16)
   - Fraud (Section 17)
   - Misrepresentation (Section 18)
   - Mistake (Section 20, 21, 22)

8. Intention to create legal relationships –

The intention of the parties to a contract must be to create a legal relationship between them. Example: A husband promising his wife to buy her a 'necklace' on occasion of her birthday is not a contract.

9. Possibility of performance –

The agreement should be capable of being performed

Example - if A promises B to bring rainfall through magic. Such agreement cannot be enforced

10. Legal formalities –

Legal formalities if any required for particular agreement such as registration, writing, they must be followed

➢ Offer –

A) Definition – Section 2(a)

When one person signifies to another his willingness to do or to abstain from doing anything, with a view to obtaining the assent of that other to such act or abstinence, he is said to make a proposal

B) Types of offer –

1. **General Offer** - It is an offer to the whole world.
2. **Specific offer** - It is an offer made to a particular person or group of persons.
3. **Express offer** - It is an offer which is made by words either oral or in writing.
4. **Implied offer** - It is an offer which is made by conduct or gesture of the parties.
5. **Counter offer** - When a person to whom the offer is made does not accept the offer [as it is] he counters the condition. This is called counter offer.
6. **Cross offer** - When two offers of same terms and conditions cross each other at same time, it is called cross offer.

7. **Standing offer** - An offer is a standing offer if it is intended to remain open for a specified period.

Essentials of valid offer –

1. **Offer may be expressed or implied –**

   An offer may be expressed or may be implied from the conduct of the parties or circumstances of the case.

2. **Offer may be specific or general –**
   a) A specific offer is one which is made to a particular person. It can be accepted by the person to whom it has been made, no one else can accept such an offer.
   b) A general offer is an offer made to the public at large.
3. **Offer must create Legal Relations –**

BASIS FOR COMPARISON	OFFER	INVITATION TO OFFER
Meaning	When one person expresses his will to another person to do or not to do something, to take his approval, is known as an offer.	When a person expresses something to another person, to invite him to make an offer, it is known as invitation to offer.
Defined in	Section 2(a) of the Indian Contract Act, 1872.	Not Defined
Objective	To enter into contract.	To receive offers from people and negotiate the terms on which the contract will be created.
Essential to make an agreement	Yes	No
Consequence	The Offer becomes an agreement when accepted.	An Invitation to offer, becomes an offer when responded by the party to whom it is made.

Harvey vs. Facey

Facts

a) Harvey was interested in buying a Jamaican property owned by Facey. He sent Facey a telegram stating "Will you sell us Bumper Hall Pen? Telegraph lowest cash price – answer paid."
b) Facey responded stating "Bumper Hall Pen £900"
c) Harvey responded stating that he would accept £900 and asking Facey to send the title deeds.
d) Facey then stated he did not want to sell.
e) Harvey sued, stating that the telegram was an offer and he had accepted, therefore there was a binding contract.
f) **Decision –**

- Telegram was an invitation to treat, not a valid offer. Therefore, no valid contract existed.
- The telegram only advised of the price, it did not explain other terms or information and therefore could not create any legal obligation.
- Harvey's telegram "accepting" the £900 was instead an offer which Facey could either accept or reject. He rejected it so there was no contract created.

➢ Acceptance

Definition – Section 2(b) **"When the person to whom an offer is made signifies his assent thereto the proposal is said to be accepted, A proposal when accepted becomes a promise."**

Essentials of valid Acceptance –

1. **Acceptance must be absolute and unqualified –**
   a) There must be an absolute and unqualified acceptance of all the terms of the offer.
   b) Qualified acceptance would amount to rejection of the offer
2. **Acceptance must be communicated –**
   Acceptance must be communicated by the acceptor
3. **Acceptance must be in a prescribed or reasonable mode –**
   a) Offer should be accepted in a prescribed mode.
   b) If the offer or prescribes no mode of acceptance, the acceptances must be communicated according in any reasonable mode such as in writing or oral.
4. **Acceptance must be given within a reasonable time and before the offer lapses –**
   a) Acceptance must be given within specified time.
   b) If no time is specified, then acceptance may be made within reasonable time.
   c) Acceptance should be made before offer lapses (expires).
5. **Acceptance cannot precede an offer –**
   a) Acceptance must be given after receiving the offer.
   b) It should not precede the offer.
6. **Acceptance must be given only by the person to whom the offer is made –**
   a) An offer can be accepted only by the person or persons to whom it is made
   b) It cannot be accepted by another person without the consent of the offeror.
7. **Rejected offer can be accepted only on renewal –**

Rejected offer can be accepted only, on renewal; offer once rejected can't be accepted again unless a fresh offer is made.

➢ COMMUNICATION OF OFFER & ACCEPTANCE AND REVOCATION – Section 4& 5

1. Communication of offer is complete when it comes to the knowledge of offeree.
2. Communication of acceptance is complete.

As against Offeror	As against Offeree
When offeree puts the acceptance in a course of transmission and it is beyond his reach to stop it.	When the acceptance comes to the knowledge of offeror.

1. **Revocation (withdrawal / cancellation) of offer** – Revocation of offer is valid before offeree puts the acceptance in course of transmission and it is out of his reach to stop it.
2. **Revocation of acceptance –** Revocation of acceptance is valid before acceptance comes to the knowledge of offeror.

Contracts over the Telephone –

- Contract over telephone can be a valid contract.
- It is important that the acceptance must be audible, heard and understood by the offeror.
- If during the conversation the telephone lines go "dead" and the offeror does not hear the offeree's word of acceptance, there is no contract at the moment.
- If the whole conversation is repeated and the offeror hears and understands the words of acceptance, the contract is complete

➢ **How revocation of proposal is made – Section 6**

• By the communication of **notice** of revocation by the proposer to the other party;
• **By the lapse of the time** prescribed in such proposal for its acceptance, or, if no time is so prescribed, by the lapse of a reasonable time, without communication of the acceptance
• By the **failure** of the acceptor **to fulfil a condition precedent** to acceptance; or
• By the **death or insanity of the proposer**, if the fact of his death or insanity comes to the knowledge of the acceptor before acceptance.
• offer **is not accepted in the prescribed mode** and if no mode is prescribed, in some usual and reasonable manner or
• The offeree makes a **counter-offer**

➢ **Consideration (quid pro quo)**

Definition – 2(d)'When at the desire of the promisor, the promisee or any other person had done or abstained from doing, or does or abstains from doing, or promises to do or to abstain from doing, something, such act or abstinence or promise is called a consideration for the promise.'

Meaning – Consideration means something in return. It may be an act or abstinence or promise

Note – As per Section 25 of the Indian Contract Act, 1872 "An agreement made without consideration is void"

Types of consideration –

Past Consideration –
In case of past consideration, the promisor had received the consideration before the date of promise

Present consideration (Executed consideration) –
Present consideration is one in which one of the parties to the contract has performed his part of the promise, which Constitutes the consideration for the promise by the other side it is known as present consideration.

Future Consideration (Executory consideration)–
when consideration is to move at a future date then it is called as future consideration

Essentials of valid consideration –

Consideration must move at the desire of the promisor –

Consideration must move at the desire of the promisor.
whatever is done must have been done at the desire of the promisor and not voluntarily or not at the desire of a third party.

Example:

- If Munna rushes to Circuit's help whose house is on fire, there is no consideration but a voluntary act. But if Munna goes to Circuit's help at Circuit's request, there is good consideration as Circuit's did not wish to do the act gratuitously (without consideration).

- Uday Bhai agrees to sell his horse to Majnu Bhai for ` 50,000. Here consideration for Uday Bhai for selling horse to Majnu Bhai is consideration of ` 50,000 from Majnu Bhai and consideration for Majnu Bhai paying ` 50,000 to Uday Bhai, is Uday Bhai selling his horse. Here considerations had come at the desire of Promisor. Uday Bhai is a promisor for Majnu Bhai and similarly Majnu Bhai is a promisor for Uday Bhai.

Consideration may move from the promisee or any other person:

a) Consideration may be furnished even by a stranger under Indian Law.
b) Consideration can be from any direction, even a stranger to contract can offer consideration. **Case law: Chinnayya v/s Ramayya.**

Chinnaya v. Ramaya, (1882) 4 Mad. 137
A lady by a deed (agreement) of gift made over certain property to her daughter directing her to pay an annuity to the donors brother as had been done by the donor herself before she gifted the property. On the same day, her daughter executed in writing in favour of the donors brother agreeing to pay the annuity. Afterwards the donee (the daughter) declined to fulfil her promise to pay her uncle saying that no consideration had moved from him. The Court, however, held that theuncle could sue even though no part of the consideration received by his niece moved from him. The consideration from her mother was sufficient consideration.

Consideration must be something of value –

Consideration must have some value in the eyes of law, and it should be real.

It may be an act, abstinence or a return promise –

a) Promise to not to smoke is a negative act (abstinence),
b) Promise to not to refer the matter to court (abstinence).
c) Promise to perform at the wedding anniversary or birthday party (promise to do).

It may be past, present or future which the promisor is already not bound to do –

d) According to Indian Law Consideration may be past, present or future.
e) But under English Law Consideration may be present or future. Past consideration is no consideration according to English Law.

It must not be unlawful –

The consideration or object of an agreement is lawful, unless —

- It is forbidden (prohibited) by law;
- or is of such a nature that, if permitted, it would defeat the provisions of any law;
- or is fraudulent;
- or involves or implies injury to the person or property of another;
- or the Court regards it as immoral, or opposed to public policy.

➢ NO CONSIDERATION – NO CONTRACT- Section 25

A) **Meaning –** The general rule is ex-nudopacto non oritur actio i.e. an agreementmade without consideration is void.

Example –

If Salman promises to pay Aishwarya ` 1000 without any obligation from Aishwarya then it will be void contract as there is no consideration from Aishwarya towards Salman.

A) Exceptions –

Under following cases, a contract will be valid even without consideration:-

1) Promise made on account of natural love and affection
2) Promise to compensate for voluntary services
3) Promise made to pay a time barred debt
4) Completed Gifts
5) Creation of agency
6) Contract of Guarantee
7) Remission.

1. Promise made on account of natural love and affection –

An agreement made without consideration is valid –

a) It is expressed in **writing**.
b) It is **registered** under the law.
c) It is made on account of **natural love and affection**.
d) It is between parties standing in **near relation** to each other.

2. Promise to compensate for voluntary services –

Voluntary service means service done without any request. It will be valid if the following conditions are satisfied –

i. The service should have been done voluntarily.
ii. The service should have been done for the promisor.
iii. The promisor must have been in existence at the time when the service was done.
iv. The intention of promisor must have been to compensate the promisee.

Example: Jethalal finds Babita's purse and gives it to 'her. Babita promises to give Jethalal 50 rupees. This is a valid contract.

3. Promise to pay time-barred debt –

i. A promise by a debtor to pay a time-barred debt is also a valid contract.
ii. But the promise must be in writing.
iii. It must be signed by the promisor or his authorised agent.
iv. The promise may be to pay the whole or part of the debt.

Example: Ram owes Laxman 1,000 rupees but the debt is barred by the Limitation Act. Ram signs a written promise to pay 500 rupees on account of the debt. The promise will be valid and binding without any fresh consideration.

4. **Creation of Agency –**
   i. No consideration is necessary to create an agency.
   ii. Thus, when a person is appointed as an agent, his appointment is valid even if there is no consideration.

5. **Completed Gifts –**
   i. Gifts once made cannot be recovered on the ground of absence of consideration.
   ii. Absence of consideration will not affect the validity of any gift already made.

Example: Virat gave a watch as a gift to Anushka on his birthday. Later on Virat cannot demand the watch back on the ground that there was no consideration.

6. **Contract of guarantee –**

Contract of guarantee needs no consideration.

7. **Remission –**

Remission means lesser performance of the contract than what is actually to be performed.
Example: Jethalal finds Babita's purse and gives it to 'her. Babita promises to give Jethalal 50 rupees. This is a valid contract.

8. **Promise to pay time-barred debt –**
   a) A promise by a debtor to pay a time-barred debt is also a valid contract.
   b) But the promise must be in writing.
   c) It must be signed by the promisor or his authorised agent.
   d) The promise may be to pay the whole or part of the debt.

Example: Ram owes Laxman 1,000 rupees but the debt is barred by the Limitation Act. Ram signs a written promise to pay 500 rupees on account of the debt. The promise will be valid and binding without any fresh consideration.

9. **Creation of Agency –**
   i. No consideration is necessary to create an agency.
   ii. Thus, when a person is appointed as an agent, his appointment is valid even if there is no consideration.

10. **Completed Gifts –**
    i. Gifts once made cannot be recovered on the ground of absence of consideration.
    ii. Absence of consideration will not affect the validity of any gift already made.

Example: Virat gave a watch as a gift to Anushka on his birthday. Later on Virat cannot demand the watch back on the ground that there was no consideration.

11. **Contract of guarantee –**
    Contract of guarantee needs no consideration.

12. Remission –

Remission means lesser performance of the contract than what is actually to be performed.

➢ DOCTRINE OF PRIVITY OF CONTRACT / STRANGER TO CONTRACT –

Exceptions – In the following cases, stranger to a contract can also sue

1. **Beneficiary of a trust –**

A trust is created for the benefit of a beneficiary. Hence, the beneficiary can enforce the provisions of the trust even though he is a stranger to the contract.

Example –In a contract between Munnabhai and Circuit, beneficial right in respect of some property may be created in favor of Chinki and in that case, Chinki can enforce his claim on the basis of this right.

2. **Provision in marriage settlement –**

A stranger to the contract can sue on the contract where a provision is made for him in marriage settlement.

3. **Provision for maintenance or marriage expenses of female members under a family arrangement** –

In case a provision is made for the marriage or maintenance of a female member of the family on the partition of a Hindu undivided family, the female member can enforce the promise though she may be a stranger to a contract.

Example –**If Nikhil gives his Property in equal portions to his 3 sons with a condition that after his death all 3 of them will give Rs 10,000 each to Neha, the daughter of Nikhil. Now Neha can prosecute if any one of them fails to obey this.**

4. **Assignee of a contract –**

The benefits of a contract may be assigned.

The assignee of a contract can enforce the benefits of a contract though he is not a party to it.

Example: Rahul assigns his insurance policy in favour of his wife. The wife can enforce it although she is not a party to it.

5. **Acknowledgement of liability –**

Where the promisor either by his conduct or acknowledgement or by part payment or by estoppel creates privity of contract between himself and the stranger, the stranger can sue.

Example: Raju pays Shyam 500 rupees to be given to Baburao, Shyam acknowledges to Baburao that he holds that amount for him. Baburao can recover the amount from Shyam.

6. **Agency contract –**

Contracts which are entered into by the agent on behalf of the principal can be enforced by the principal even though he is not a party to the contract.

➢ Free consent

Meaning - Section 13 'Two or more persons are said to consent when they agree upon the same thing in the same sense.'

When consent is said to be free

As per section 14 of the Contract act consent is said to be free when **following are absent** -

Coercion (Section 15)	Undue influence (Section 16)	Fraud (Section 17)	Misrepresentation (Section 18)	Mistake (Section 20,21, 22)

Coercion - Section 15

Meaning of coercion -

1. Committing or threatening to commit any act forbidden (prohibited) by Indian Penal Code against another person; or
2. Unlawful detaining or threatening to detain the property of another person with a view to obtain consent of another person.

a) Who can exercise coercion -

Coercion may come from a person party to the contract or even third person not connected with the contract directly.

b) **Important points** -

Prosecution - A mere (only) threat to prosecute a man or file suit against him does not constitute a coercion.

High prices and high interest Rates - Charging high interest rate, high price etc. is not a coercion as the same is not prohibited under the Indian Penal code.

A threat to commit suicide - Consent to an agreement may at times be obtained by threatening to commit suicide. Threat to commit suicide also amounts to coercion.

c) What will be the effect if the consent is caused by coercion - **Section 19**

- Agreement is voidable at the **option of aggrieved party**.
- Aggrieved party has the option to cancel (rescind) the contract.
- If the aggrieved party decides to rescind the contract, he must return (restore) all the benefits received by such person.

- **Undue Influence - Section 16**

Meaning of undue influence –

- A contract is said to be induced (caused) by "undue influence" where the relations subsisting (existing) between the parties are such that one of the parties is in a position to dominate the will of the other and uses that position to obtain an unfair advantage over the other.

A. When a person is deemed to be in a dominating position?

- Where he holds a real or apparent authority over the other (e.g. master and servant) where he stands in a fiduciary (trust) relation to the other (e.g. Doctor and patient)
- Where he makes a contract with a person whose mental capacity is temporarily or permanently affected by reason of age, illness, or mental or bodily distress (pain)

Note – **The burden of proving that the contract was not induced by undue influence shall lie upon the person in a position to dominate the will of the other**

B. There is presumption of undue influence in the following relationships –

a) Parent and child
b) Guardian and ward
c) Doctor and patient
d) Solicitor and client
e) Trustee and beneficiary
f) Religious advisor and disciple
g) Fiancé and fiancée

C. However, there is no presumption of undue influence in case of relationship of

h) landlord and tenant
i) debtor and creditor
j) husband and wife.

D. What will be the effect if the consent is caused by Undue influence – Section 19

k) Agreement is voidable at the option of aggrieved party.
l) Aggrieved party has the option to cancel (rescind) the contract.
m) If the aggrieved party decides to rescind the contract, he must return (restore) all the benefits received by such person

➢ Fraud Section 17

Meaning of fraud –

- "Fraud" means and includes any of the following acts committed by a party to a contract, or with his connivance, or by his agent, with intent to deceive another party or his agent, or to induce him to enter into the contract:
  a. The suggestion, as a fact, of that which is not true by one who does not believe it to be true;

b. The active concealment (to hide) of a fact by one having knowledge or belief of the fact;
c. A promise made without any intention of performing it;
d. Any other act fitted to deceive;
e. Any such act which the law specially declares to be fraudulent

Note -Deceive - intentionally cause (someone) to believe something that is not true Connivance - willingness for being secretly involved in an immoral or illegal act.

A) Is silence fraud?

a) Whether silence is fraud or not depends upon various factors.
b) Normally speaking, silence does not amount to fraud.
c) However, silence will be considered as fraud in the following situations -

- When there is a duty to speak
- Where silence is equivalent to speech.
- Where there is change in circumstances

B) What will be the effect if the consent is caused by Fraud - Section 19

a) Agreement is voidable at the option of aggrieved party.
b) Aggrieved party has the option to cancel (rescind) the contract.
c) If aggrieved party decides not to cancel the contract then he may continue the contract and claim damages from the other party.
d) If the aggrieved party decides to rescind the contract, he must return (restore) all the benefits received by such person.

Contracts Uberrimae Fidei -
There are contracts in which the law imposes a special duty to act with the utmost good faith i.e., to disclose all material information. Failure to disclose such information will render the contract voidable at the option of the other party
Examples -

A) Contract of insurance of all kinds
B) Company prospectus
C) Contract for the sale of land
D) Contracts of family arrangement

- **Misrepresentation - Section 18**

Meaning: A representation when wrongly made either innocently or intentionally is misrepresentation. When it is made innocently or unintentionally it is misrepresentation and when made intentionally or willfully it is fraud.

- Misrepresentation means making any statement as true but actually that statement is false.

What will be the effect if the consent is caused by Undue influence – Section 19

- Agreement is voidable at the option of aggrieved party.
- Aggrieved party has the option to cancel (rescind) the contract.
- If the aggrieved party decides to rescind the contract, he must return (restore) all the benefits received by such person

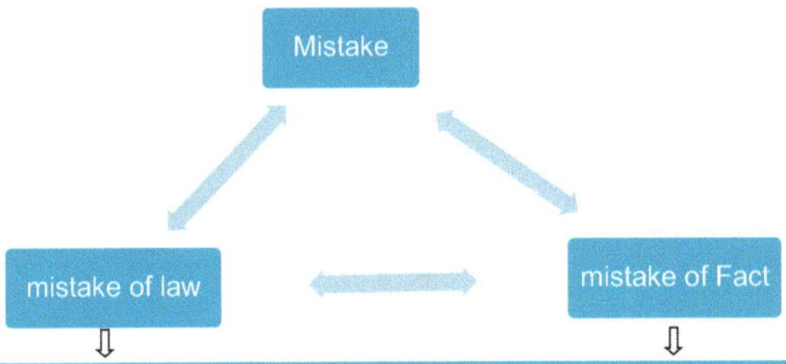

Indian Law	Foreign Law	Bilateral law	unbilateral law
Valid	Void	Void	Valid

Mistake of law – Section 21

Mistake of law of the country –

1) When a partynters into a contract, without the knowledge of law in the country, the **contract is valid and not void.**
2) A contract is not voidable because it was caused by a mistakeas to any law in force in India.
3) The reason here is that **Ignorantia juris non excusat (ignorance of law is not an excuse at all).**
4) However, if a party is induced (influenced) to enter into a contract by the mistake of law then such a contract may be avoided.
5) The principle in this case is ignorance of law is not an excuse.

Mistake of law of foreign country –

1) Such a mistake is treated as mistake of fact and agreement is such case is void.
2) **Ignorance of foreign law may be excused**

➤ ***Mistake of fact – Section***

A) **Bilateral mistake** -

1) Where both the parties to an agreement are under a mistake as to a matter of fact essential to the agreement, the agreement is void.
2) Mistake must be mutual i.e. both the parties should misunderstand each other

Types of mistakes falling under bilateral mistake are as follows –

(a) **Mistake as to existence of subject matter:** If both the parties are at mutual mistake as to existence of the subject matter the agreement is void.
(b) **Mistake as to identity of subject matter:** It usually happens when both the parties have different subject matter of contract in their mind. The contract is void due to mistake of identify of subject matter.
(c) **Mistake as to the quality of the subject matter:** If the subject matter is something essentially different from what the parties thought to be, the agreement is void.
(d) **Mistake as to quantity of subject matter:** Bilateral mistake as to quantity of subject matter would render the contract void.

(e) **Mistake as to title of subject matter:** The agreement is void due to bilateral mistake as to title of the subject matter.

(f) **Mistake as to price of the subject matter:** Mutual mistake as to price of the subject matter would render the agreement void.

(g) **Mistake as to possibility of performance of Contract** - Impossibility may be:
Physical impossibility: A contract is void if it is identified to be non-feasible (not possible) due to physical factors, like time, distance, height, etc.
Legal impossibility: A contract is void if it provides that something shall be done which as a matter of law cannot be done.

B) **Unilateral Mistake as to fact – Section 22**

1) A contract is not voidable merely because it was caused by one of the parties to it being under a mistake as to a matter of fact.
2) A unilateral mistake is not allowed as a defense in avoiding a contract unless the mistakes brought about by another party's fraud or misrepresentation.

➢ Legality of Object – Section 23

Section 23 of the Indian Contract Act, 1872 provides that the consideration or object of an agreement is unlawful if it is –

- **forbidden by law**; or
- it is of such nature that **if permitted it would defeat the provisions of law**; or
- is **fraudulent**; or
- involves or implies **injury to the person or property** of another; or
- the Court regards it as **immoral or opposed to public policy**.

In each of these cases the consideration or object of an agreement is said to be unlawful. Every agreement of which the object or consideration is unlawful is void

➢ Void and Illegal Contract

Consequence of Illegal Agreements

- an illegal agreement **is entirely void**;
- **no action can be brought** by a party to the contract to an illegal agreement. The maxim is **"Ex turpi cause non-oritur action" - from an evil cause, no action arises;**
- money paid or property transferred under an illegal agreement cannot be recovered. The maxim is **in parti delicto potierest condition defendeties- In cases of equal guilt, more powerful is the condition of the defendant;**
- where an agreement consist of two parts, one part legal and other illegal, and the legal parts is separable from the illegal one, then the Court will enforce the legal one. If the legal and the illegal parts cannot be separated the whole agreement is illegal; and
- any agreement which is collateral (connected) to an illegal agreement is also tainted with illegality and is treated as being illegal, even though it would have been lawful by itself.

➢ Agreements Void as being opposed to Public Policy –

The following agreements are void as being against public policy but they are not illegal –

a. **Agreement in restrain (restrict) of parental rights** An agreement by which a party deprives himself of the custody of his child is void.
b. **Agreement in restraint of marriage** : An agreement not to marry at all or not to marry any particular person or class of persons is void as it is in restraint of marriage.
c. **Marriage brokerage or brokerage Agreements** : An agreement to procure marriage for reward is void. Where a purohit (priest) was promised Rs.200 in consideration of procuring a wife for the defendant, the promise was held void as opposed to public policy, and the purohit could not recover the promised sum.
d. **Agreements in restraint of personal freedom are void** : Where a man agreed with his money lender not to change his residence, or his employment or to part with any of his property or to incur any obligation on credit without the consent of the money lender, it was held that the agreement was void.
e. **Agreement in restraint of trade** : An agreement in restraint of trade is one which seeks to restrict a person from freely exercising his trade or profession.

➢ Agreements Void as being opposed to Public Policy------------------

The following agreements are void as being against public policy but they are not illegal –

a) **Agreement in restrain (restrict) of parental rights** : An agreement by which a party deprives himself of the custody of his child is void.
b) **Agreement in restraint of marriage** : An agreement not to marry at all or not to marry any particular person or class of persons is void as it is in restraint of marriage.
c) **Marriage brokerage or brokerage Agreements** : An agreement to procure marriage for reward is void. Where a purohit (priest) was promised Rs.200 in consideration of procuring a wife for the defendant, the promise was held void as opposed to public policy, and the purohit could not recover the promised sum.
d) **Agreements in restraint of personal freedom are void** : Where a man agreed with his money lender not to change his residence, or his employment or to part with any of his property or to incur any obligation on credit without the consent of the money lender, it was held that the agreement was void.
e) **Agreement in restraint of trade** : An agreement in restraint of trade is one which seeks to restrict a person from freely exercising his trade or profession.

➢ Void Agreements –

Following agreements have been expressly declared to be void by the Indian Contract Act –

- Agreement made by incompetent person	- Agreement in restraint of marriage – Section 26
- Agreement made under a bilateral mistake of fact – Section 20	- Agreement in restraint of trade – Section 27
- Agreement of which the consideration or object is unlawful – Section 23	- Agreement in restraint of legal proceedings – Section 28
- Agreement of which the consideration or object is unlawful in part – Section 24	- Agreements void for uncertainty – Section 29
- Agreement made without consideration – Section 25	- Wagering agreement
- Agreement to do impossible acts	

a) Agreement by a minor (section 11) or a person of unsound mind (section 12).
b) Agreement of which the consideration or object is unlawful – Section 23
c) Agreement made under a bilateral mistake of fact material to the agreement – Section 20
d) Agreement of which the consideration or object is unlawful in part and the illegal part cannot be separated from the legal part – Section 24
e) **Agreement in restraint of marriage – Section 26**

   Agreement is restraint of marriage is void.

   Exceptions: a) Minors; b) Restraint for particular reasonable period is valid
f) **Agreement in restraint of trade is void.**

   Exceptions –
   - An agreement through which an **outgoing partner** will not carry on the business of the firm for a reasonable time will be valid, though it is in restraint of trade
   - Where a person **sells his business along with the goodwill** to another person, agrees not to carry on same line of business in certain reasonable local limits, such an agreement is valid.
   - An **agreement of service** through which an employee commits not to compete with his employer is not in restraint of trade
   - Trade **Combinations** are valid as long as they are not creating monopoly are valid
g) **Agreement in restraint of legal proceedings – Section 28**

   An agreement which restricts or waives one's right to sue or limits the time of justice is void.

Exceptions:

- A contract by which the parties agree that any dispute between them shall be referred to arbitration and will not be taken to the court is a valid contract.

h) **Agreements void for uncertainty – Section 29**

Agreements, the meaning of which is not certain, or capable of being made certain are void.

i) **Agreement by way of wager – Section 30**

Payment of money or money's worth upon ascertainment of future uncertain event isknown as wagering.

➢ Wagering Agreements –

Meaning of wagering agreements –

The literal meaning of the word "wager" is a "bet". Wageringagreements are nothing but ordinary betting agreements.

Example -A and B enter into an agreement that if England's Cricket Team winsthe test match, A will pay B Rs.100 and if it loses B will pay Rs.100 to A. This is a wagering agreement and nothing can be recovered bywinning party under the agreement.

A) **Essentials of wagering agreements –**
   a) **One party should win and one part should loose**
   b) **There should be mutual chance of gain or loss**
   c) **No parties should have control over the event.**

➢ Performance of contract

Meaning – Every contract has certain obligations (duties) which are to be performed by the parties to thecontract.

- When both the parties to the Contract fulfill their obligations towards each other, the contract issaid to be performed.
- When both the parties to the contract have performed their obligations, the contract is said tobe discharged by performance.

Who will perform the contract? - Section 40

- Promisor himself
- Legal Representative However, if the contract involves personal skills and if the promisor dies, the
- Agent of promisor
- Third persons, if promise permits

Example -Adi promises to pay Manav 5,000 rupees. Adi may perform the obligation of giving 5,000 rupees to Manav either by himself or he may appoint agent to perform the obligation.
If Adi dies before making the payment then legal repetitive of Adi must perform the promise.

➢ Effect of Refusal to accept offer of performance -Section 38

When the promisor make offer to the promise for the performance of the contract and promise does not accept it, then the promisor is not responsible for non-performance

Conditions –

1. It must be **unconditional**
2. Performance must be at a **proper time and place**
3. Performance must be within **reasonable time**.
4. Performance must give reasonable **opportunity for inspection**

⇩

Example:
Jay contracts to deliver to Veeru at his warehouse 100 Kg of Basmati rice of A grade quality on the 1st March, 2014,. In order to make an offer of a performance as per section 38, Jay must bring the rice to Veeru's warehouse, on the fixed date (1st March, 2014), under such circumstances that Veeru may have a reasonable opportunity of satisfying himself that the thing offered is Basmati rice of the quality contracted for, and that there are 100 kg of rice.

➢ Effect of Refusal of Party to Perform Promise Wholly - Section 39

a) If the promisor refuses to perform the contract wholly, the promisee may put an end to the contract.
b) However, if the promisee has agreed to accept the performance even if it is not performed wholly then the contract will continue.

Example
Kanika Kapoor, a singer, enters into a contract with Neha Dhupia, the manager of a theatre, to sing at his theatre two nights in every week during the next two months, and Neha Dhupia promises to pay her 100 rupees for each night's performance. On the sixth night Kanika willfully absents herself from the theatre. Neha is at liberty to put an end to the contract and it depends on her choice

➢ Effect of accepting performance from third person - Section 41

When a promisee accepts performance of the promise from a third person, he cannot afterwards enforce it against the promisor.

Narendra and Rahul enter into a contract in which Narendra will supply raw materials to Rahul. The raw material of Narendra is in Chennai's warehouse which is managed by Mr. Shah. Narendra gave direction to Mr Shah to deliver raw material to Rahul which Mr Shah did and it was accepted by Rahul. Now, Rahul cannot demand delivery of raw materials from Narendra.

➢ Devolution (transfer) of Joint Liabilities - Section 42 and 43 and 44

- Liability of joint promisor is joint and several
- If any joint promisor dies, his legal representatives must jointly with the surviving promisors fulfil the promise.
- On the death of all the joint promisors, the representatives of all of them must jointly fulfil the promise.
- The promisee may compel (force) anyone of the joint promisor to perform the promise –

Section 43

- Where a promisee releases one of the joint promisors, the release of one promisor does not discharge the other joint promisors – **Section 44**

- **Note –Each promisor may compel contribution–**

  Everyone will contribute equally or as per the terms and conditions agreed between the joint promisor.

  - **Sharing of loss by default in contribution**–

  If any one of two or more joint promisors makes default in such contribution, the remaining joint promisors must bear the loss arising from such default in equal shares.

Examples:1. Raju, Shyam and Baburao jointly promise to pay Totla Seth ` 3,000. Totla Seth may compel (force) either Raju or Shyam or Baburao to pay him ` 3,000.

2. Raju, Shyam and Baburao jointly promise to pay Totla Seth the sum of ` 3,000. Baburao is compelled to pay the whole.

3. Raju is insolvent, but his assets are sufficient to pay one-half of his debts, Baburao is entitled to receive ` 500 from Raju's estate, and ` 1,250 from Shyam.

4. Raju, Shyam and Baburao are under a joint promise to pay Totla Seth ` 3,000. Baburao is unable to pay anything, and Raju is compelled to pay the whole. Raju is entitled to receive ` 1,500 from Shyam.

5. Raju, Shyam and Baburao are under a joint promise to pay Totla Seth ` 3,000, Raju and Shyam being only sureties (guarantor) for Baburao. Baburao fails to pay. Raju and Shyam are compelled to pay the whole sum. They are entitled to recover it from Baburao.

➢ Devolution of Joint Rights (Section 45)

When a person has made a promise to two or more persons jointly then the right to claim performance rests with all the joint promisee and if any of the joint promisee dies then the legal representative of that joint promisee along with the surviving joint promisee shall claim the performance. If all the joint promise die the legal representative of all joint promisee shall claim the performance.

Bhuvam, in consideration of ` 5,000, lent to him by Ashish and Carry, promises Ashish and Carry jointly to repay them 5,000 with interest on a day specified, but Ashish dies.

The right to claim performance rests with Ashish's representative jointly with Carry during Carry's life, and after the death of Carry with the representatives of Ashish and Carry jointly.

➢ Time and place for performance of contract - Section 46-50

1) **Time for Performance of Promise, where no application is to be made and no time is specified - Section 46**

Where the promise is to be performed without application by the promisee and no time for the performance is specified then the contract shall be performed within reasonable time.
Reasonable time differs case to case and if there is any dispute then court will decide the reasonable time.

2) **Time and Place for Performance of Promise, where time is specified and no application to be made - Section 47**

Where the promise is to be performed on fixed day without application by the promisee then the promisor may perform the promise on that day during business hours and on such place as specified.

> **Example:**
> Mukesh promises to deliver goods at Rahul's warehouse on the 1st January. On that day Mukesh brings the goods to Rahul's warehouse, but after the usual hour for closing it, and they are not received. Mukesh has not performed his promise.

3) **Application for Performance on certain day to be at proper time and place - Section 48**

When a promise is to be performed on a certain day and for that promisee has to make application to promisor then it is the duty of the promisee to apply for performance at a proper place and within the usual hours of business.

4) **Place for Performance of Promise, where no application to be made and no place fixed for performance - Section 49**

When a promise is to be performed without application by the promisee and place of performance is not fixed then it is the duty of the promisor to apply to the promisee to appoint a reasonable place for the performance of the promise.

5) **Performance in Manner or at time prescribed or Sanctioned by Promisee - Section 50**

Where promisee specifies the manner or time of performance then promisor should perform promise in the manner or time specified by the promisee.

➢ Performance of Reciprocal Promises - Section 51 - 54 and 57

1) **Simultaneous performance - Section 51**

Promises are to be performed together by the promisor as well as promisee.

Example: Kabir and Priti contract that Kabir shall deliver goods to Priti and Priti will pay the price for the goods. Kabir need not deliver the goods, unless Priti is ready and willing to pay for the goods on delivery. Priti need not pay for the goods, unless Kabir is ready and willing to deliver them on payment.

2) **Order of performance - Section 52**

promises should be performed in the fixed order and if no order is fixed then it can be performed in any manner

Example: A and B contract that A shall build a house for B at a fixed price and B shall make the payment after the house is ready. A's promise to build the house must be performed before B's promise to pay for it.

3) **Liability of party preventing event on which the contract is to take effect – Section 53**

Where one party to a reciprocal promise prevents the other party from performing his promise, the contract becomes voidable at the option of the party who is so prevented. The aggrieved party can also recover compensation.

Example: Karan and Amir contract that Karan shall execute certain work for Amir for 200 rupees. Karan is ready to perform the work, but Amir prevents him from doing so. The contract is voidable at the option of Karan; and, if Karan elects to rescind the contract then Karan is entitled to recover from Amir compensation for any loss which he has incurred by its non-performance

4) **Conditional and dependent – Section 54**

Legal and Illegal Reciprocal Promises – Section 57

legal part → Valid

illegal part → Void

NOTE – But if the things are inseparable then the entire agreement is void

Time is Essence of the Contract – Section 55

Effect of failure to perform at a fixed time in a contract in which time is essential –

When the element of **time is not essential** in the contract

↓

if the promisor fails to perform the Contract within the fixed period

Promisee has 2 options

Option 1

↓

Promisee can affirm (accept) the contract

Option 2

↓

Promisee can rescind (cancel) the contract and **can**

When the element of **time is essential** in the contract

↓

if the promisor fails to perform the contract within the fixed period.

In this case promise can only damage

claim and can claim
Damages
to the promisor

damages if he notifies

➢ Agreement to do impossible acts – Section 56

1. An agreement to do an act impossible in itself is void.
2. Contract to do an act afterwards becoming impossible or unlawful —A contract to do an act which, after the contract is made, becomes impossible or unlawful, or, by reason of some event which the promisor could not prevent, becomes void when the act becomes impossible or unlawful.
3. In such cases, promisor should compensate promisee for any loss.

a) A agrees with B to discover treasure by magic. The agreement is void

b) Hitesh and Makarand contract to marry each other. Before the time fixed for the marriage,. Hitesh goes mad. The contract becomes void

c) A contracts to take in cargo for B at a foreign port. A's Government afterwards declares war against the country in which the port is situated. The contract becomes void when war is declared.

➢ Appropriation of payments – Section 59,60 and 61

Where a debtor owes several debts to creditors then the provisions of section 59-61 comes into picture

There can be 3 situations for settlement of debt if debtor owes several debt to creditor

Situation 1	Situation 2	Situation 3
Where the debtor has Specified – **Section 59** Follow the instructions Of debtor and adjust the Debt accordingly	where the creditor has specified – **Section 60** Follow the instructions of creditors and adjust the debt accordingly	where no one has specified **Section – 61** Debt should be appropriated as per time. However, if 2 loans are taken on same day the appropriation must be done proportionately

Examples:

1.Ranveer owes Ranbir several debts including, 1,000 rupees upon a promissory note which falls due on the 1st June. He owes Ranbir no other debt of that amount. On the 1st June Ranveer pays to Ranbir ` 1,000. The payment is to be applied to the discharge of the promissory note.

2.Ranveer owes to Ranbir several debts, the sum of ` 567. Ranbir writes to Ranveer and demands payment of this sum. Ranveer sends to Ranbir ` 567. This payment is to be applied to the discharge of the debt of which Ranbir had demanded payment.

➢ Quasi Contracts - Section 68-72

Meaning of quasi contract -

1) **It is an implied contract.** It is imposed by law and does not arise by agreement
2)  The duty of a party and not the promise of any party is the basis of such contract.
3) **It is based on the principle of "prevention of unjust enrichment of one person at the cost of another"**
4) It is imposed by law and does not arise by agreement.
5) No essential of valid contract is required
6) The right is available against specific persons and not the whole world.

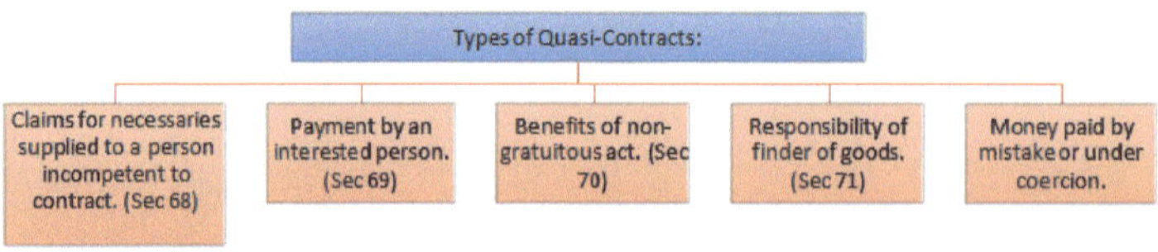

➢ Claims for necessaries supplied - Section 68

Where necessaries are supplied to a person who is incompetent to contract, the supplier is entitled to recover the price from the property of the incompetent person.

➢ Example: Gopal supplies Madhav, a minor, with necessaries suitable to his condition in life. Gopal is entitled to be reimbursed from Madhav's property.

➢ Payment by a Person Having Some Interest in Payment - Section 69

a) The person making the payment must have some interest in paying the amount.

The person making the A person who is interested in the payment of money of which another is bound (liable) by law to pay, and who therefore, pays it, is entitled to be reimbursed by the other **Conditions**:

b) payment must not be bound by law to pay the amount.
c) The other person from whom the money is sought to be recovered must be legally bound to pay the money.

C) Claim for any benefit received under a non-gratuitous act – Section 70

When a person lawfully does anything for another person or delivers anything to him, not intending to do so gratuitously, such person who enjoys the benefit must reimburse the former or must restore to him the thing so delivered.

Conditions:

a) The person must lawfully do something for another person or deliver something to him.
b) The person doing some act or delivering something must not intend to act gratuitously
c) The other person must voluntarily accept the acts or goods and he must have enjoyed their benefits

D) Responsibility of finder of goods – Section 71

A person who finds goods belonging to another and takes them into his custody is liable as a bailee. The finder of goods must try to find out the real owner of the goods and deliver the goods to him on demand.

E) Money paid by mistake or under coercion – Section 72

A person to whom money has been paid or anything delivered by mistake or under coercion, must repay or return it.

Example: Ram and Shyam jointly owe 1,000 rupees to Malinga. Ram alone pays the amount to Malinga, and Shyam, not knowing this fact, later on also pays 1,000 to Malinga. Malinga is bound to repay the amount to B.

➤ Contingent Contract – Section 31-36

A contract may be

Absolute contract - it is a type of contract where the promisor promises to the perform the contract without conditions. It is also known as unconditional **contract**	**Contingent contract-** it is a type of contract where performance is dependent on some conditions which may happen or may not happen

A) Section 31 defines contingent contract as follows –

"a contract to do or not to do something if some event, collateral to such contract, does or does not happen"

Example –Vasuli Bhai contracts to pay Bappi Bhai 5 lakh rupees if Bappi Bhai's house is burnt. This is a contingent contract.

Contracts of insurance, indemnity and guarantee are also example of contingent contracts.

B) Essentials of Contingent Contract –

a) There must be a contract to do or not to do something
b) The performance of the contract depends upon the happening or non-happening of some event in future
c) The event must be uncertain (not fixed)
d) The event must be collateral or incidental to the contract

C) Rules regarding contingent contract –

1) Enforcement of contingent contracts on an event happening – Section 32

Contracts which are contingent upon the happening of a future uncertain event cannot be enforced by law unless and until that event has happened. If the event becomes impossible, such contracts become void.

Example:

a) Alex promises to pay Peter 5,000 rupees if the ship reaches port. Now, contract will be enforceable (valid) if ship reaches the port. On the other hand if ship does not reaches port then contract will be void.

b) Janvi contracts to pay Hitesh a sum of 1 lakh rupees when Hitesh marries Makarand. Makarand dies without being married to Hitesh. The contract becomes void.

2) Enforcement of contracts contingent on an event not happening – Section 33

Contracts contingent upon the non-happening of an uncertain future event can be enforced when the happening of that event becomes impossible

Example: Alex agrees to pay Peter a sum of 10 lakh rupees if a certain ship does not return. The ship is sunk. The contract can be enforced after the ship sinks. On the other hand, if ship would have returned the contract would have become void.

3) Contingent Contracts Dependent on future conduct of a living person – Section 34

If the future event on which a contract is contingent is dependent on the future act of a living person then contract will become void if that person acts otherwise

Example – Sharvi agrees to pay Makarand 1 lakh rupees if Makarand marries Hitesh. Hitesh marries Gaurang. The marriage of Makarand to Hitesh must now be considered impossible, although it is possible that Gaurang may die and that Hitesh may afterwards marry Makarand.

4) When contracts become void which are contingent on happening of specified event within fixed time – Section 35

Contracts which are contingent upon the happening of a future uncertain event within a fixed time will becomes void if the contract does not happen within fixed time.

Example –

a) Alex promises to pay Peter 5,000 rupees if the ship reaches port within 1 year. Now, contract will be enforceable (valid) if ship reaches the port within one year. On the other hand, if ship does not reach port within 1 year then contract will be void.
b) Alex promises to pay Peter 5,000 rupees if the ship does not reach port within 1 year. Now, contract will be enforceable (valid) if ship does not reach the port within one year. On the other hand, if ship reaches port within 1 year then contract will be void.

5) Agreements contingent on impossible events void – Section 36

Contingent agreements based on impossible event are void.

Example – Anuradha promised Shyam to pay 1 crore rupees if he brings Taj Mahal from Delhi to Mumbai. This contract is void contract.

➤ Discharge of contract –

Meaning of Discharge of contract – Discharge of contract means termination of contractual relationship between the parties. In simple words discharge of contract means that contract comes to an end.

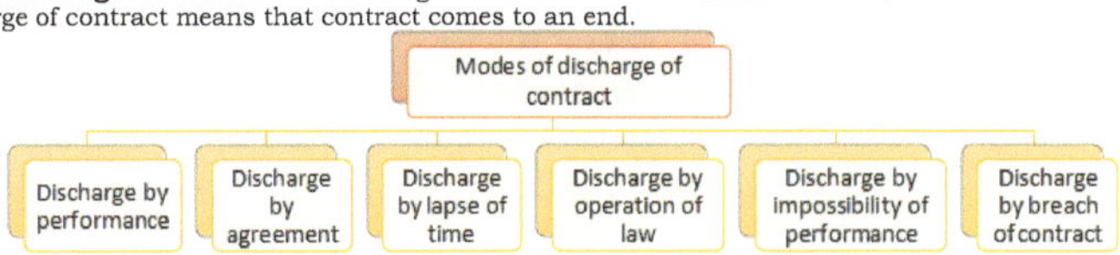

➤ Discharge by performance –

When the parties to a contract fulfil the obligations arising under the contract within the time and manner prescribed, then the contract is discharged by performance.

Example: Peter agrees to sell his cycle to John for an amount of Rs 10,000 to be paid by John on the delivery of the cycle. As soon as it is delivered, John pays the promised amount.

Since both the parties to the contract fulfil their obligation arising under the contract, then it is discharged by performance.

Discharge by agreement

The parties may agree to terminate the existence of the contract by any of the following ways:

1) **Novation - Section 62**
   a) Substitution of a new contract in place of the existing contract is known as "Novation ofContract".
   b) It discharges the original contract.
   c) The new contract may be between the same parties or between different parties.
   d) Novation can take place only with the consent of all the parties.

   Example: Raju owes money to Shyam under a contract. It is agreed between Raju, Shyam and Baburao that Shyam should accept Baburao as his debtor, instead of Raju. The old debt of Raju and Shyam is at an end and a new debt from Baburao to Shyam has been contracted. There is novation involving change of parties.

2) **Alteration - Section 62**
   a) Alteration means change in one or more of the terms of thecontract.
   a) In case of novation there may be a change of the parties, while in the case of alteration, the parties remain the same.
   b) But there is a change in the terms of the contract.
   c) Alteration can take place only with the consent of all the parties

3) **Rescission - Section 62**
   It means the cancellation of the contract.

4) **Remission – Section 63**
   It means the acceptance of lesser fulfilment of the terms of the promise
   Example: Salman has borrowed ` 500 from Aishwarya. Salman agrees to accept ` 250 from Aishwarya in satisfaction of the whole debt. The whole debt is discharged.

5) Waiver - Section 63 Waiver means giving up or foregoing certain rights. When a party agrees to give up its rights, the contract is discharged.

Example: A promises to paint a picture of B. B afterwards forbids him to do so. A is no longerbound to perform the promise.

➤ Discharge of a Contract by Lapse of Time

The Limitation Act, 1963 prescribes a specified period for performance of contract. If the promisor fails to perform and the promisee fails to take action within this specified period, then the promisee cannot seek remedy through law. It dischargesthe contract due to the lapse of time.

Example: Peter takes a loan from John and agrees to pay instalments every month for the next five years. However, he does not pay even a single instalment. John callshim a few times but then gets busy and takes no action. Three years later, he approaches the court to help him recover his money. However, the court rejects his suit since he has crossed the time-limit of three years to recover his debts.

D) Discharge by operation of law –

A contract may be discharged by operation of law in the following cases –

1) **Death** –
   a) If contract involves personal skill then contract is discharged
   b) If contract does not involve personal skill then the rights and liabilities of the deceasedperson will pass on to his legal representatives.
2) **Insolvency** –
   The insolvency of the promisor discharges the contract
3) **Unauthorized material alteration** –
   Material alteration in the terms of the contract without the consent of the other partydischarges the contract.
4) **Merger** –
   When inferior rights of a person under a contract merge with superior rights under a new contract, the contract with inferior rights will come to an end. Examples: Where a part-time lecturer is made full-time lecturer, merger discharges the contract of part-time lecturer ship.

E) Discharge by breach of contract –

Breach means failure of a party to perform his obligations under a contract. Breach brings an end to the obligations created by a contract.

F) Discharge by impossibility of performance –

Impossibility of performance results in the discharge of the contract. An agreement which is impossible is void, because law does not compel to do impossible things.

Example: A and B wanted to marry each other. Before the time fixed formarriage, A goes mad. The contract becomes void.

➢ Breach of Contract and Remedies for breach of contract Section 73-75

Meaning of breach of contract –

➢ When a promise or agreement is broken by any of the parties, we call it a breach of contract. So when either of the parties does not keep their end of the agreement or does not fulfil their obligation as per the terms of the contract, it is a breach of contract. **Breach of contract can be actual breach or anticipatory breach.**

A) Anticipatory Breach of Contract

As the name suggests, an anticipatory breach is a breach of contract before the time of performance. So, if a promisor denies to perform his promise and signifies his unwillingness before the time for performance, then it is an anticipatory breach of contract.

Examples –

a) Peter enters into a contract with John on May 30, 2018. In the contract, Peter agrees to sell his house to John provided he receives a token amount of Rs 5,00,000 from John on or before June 30, 2018. However, on June 15, 2018, John informs Peter that he will not be able to provide the token amount on the said date, thereby expressing rejection of the contract.

b) . Peter enters into a contract with John on June 01, 2018. As per the contract, Peter agrees to sell his guitar to John on June 10, 2018, for an amount of Rs 5,000. However, he sells this guitar to Oliver on June 07, 2018. Hence, it is an anticipatory breach of contract due to Peter's conduct.

When a promisor refuses to perform his promise leading to an anticipatory breach of contract, the promisee is excused from performance or from further performance of his obligations. Also, he can either:

- **Treat the contract as cancelled and file a suit against the other party for damages** arising from the breach. This suit can be filed immediately without waiting until the date of performance specified in the contract.

  OR

- **Choose not to cancel the contract but treat it as an operative** and wait until the time of performance has passed before holding the other party responsible for the damages caused due to non- performance.

➢ Actual Breach of Contract

While an anticipatory breach is before the time of performance, an actual breach of contract is on the scheduled time of performance of the contract. An actual breach of contract can be committed either:

1] At the time when the Performance of the Contract is Due

Peter enters into a contract with John promising to deliver 50 bags of cotton to him on June 30, 2018. However, on the scheduled day, he fails to deliver the same. This is an actual breach of contract. Also, this breach is at the time the performance of the contract is due.

2] During the Performance of the Contract

An actual breach of contract can also occur when one party fails to perform his obligation, during theperformance of the contract. This refusal can be expressed in words or by action.

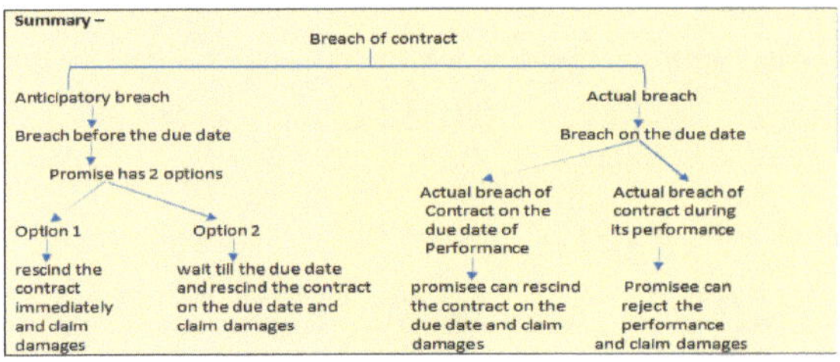

Following are the remedies for the breach of contract –

A) Recession of Contract

When one of the parties to a contract does not fulfil his obligations, then the other party can rescind the contract and refuse the performance of his obligations.

As per section 65 of the Indian Contract Act, the party that rescinds the contract must restore any benefits he got under the said agreement. And section 75 states that the party that rescinds the contract is entitled to receive damages and/or compensation for such a recession

B) Sue for Damages

Section 73 clearly states that the party who has suffered, since the other party has broken promises, can claim compensation for loss or damages caused to them in the normal course of business.

Such damages will not be payable if the loss is abnormal in nature, i.e. not in the ordinary course ofbusiness. There are two types of damages according to the Act,

- **Liquidated damages -** Sometimes the parties to a contract will agree to the amount payable in case of a breach. This is known as liquidated damages.
- **Unliquidated Damages -** Here the amount payable due to the breach of contract is assessed by the courts or any appropriate authorities.

C) **Sue for Specific Performance**

This means the party in breach will actually have to carry out his duties according to the contract. In certain cases, the courts may insist that the party carry out the agreement.

So if any of the parties fails to perform the contract, the court may order them to do so. This is a decree of specific performance and is granted instead of damages.

For example, A decided to buy a parcel of land from B. B then refuses to sell. The courts can order B to perform his duties under the contract and sell the land to A.

D) **Injunction**

An injunction is basically like a decree for specific performance but for a negative contract. An injunction is a court order restraining a person from doing a particular act.

So, a court may grant an injunction to stop a party of a contract from doing something he promised not to do. In a prohibitory injunction, the court stops the commission of an act and in a mandatory injunction, it will stop the continuance of an act that is unlawful.

E) **Quantum Meruit**

Quantum meruit literally translates to "as much is earned". At times when one party of the contract is prevented from finishing his performance of the contract by the other party, he can claim quantum meruit.

So he must be paid a reasonable remuneration for the part of the contract he has already performed. This could be the remuneration of the services he has provided or the value of the work he has already done.

➢ LANDMARK JUDGEMENTS

❖ ***Balfour v. Balfour (1919)***

The 1919 case of **Balfour v. Balfour** was the foundation for the contract law as it gave birth to the purpose behind the creation of the legal reaction theory in contract law. Legal reaction theory means that one lawful act will be responsible for a subsequent legal act to take place. Lord Justice Atkin observed that agreements that are made between a husband and his wife, specifically personal family relationships, to provide maintenance costs, and other related capitals are generally not categorized as contracts because in general, the parties to the agreement do not intend to enter into an agreement that should be attending legal ends. Therefore, a contract cannot be enforceable by nature if the parties to the same do not intend to create legal relations with each other.

❖ ***Lal man Shukla v. Gauri Datt (1913)***

The importance of knowledge and communication, in formation of a contract, was highlighted by the Allahabad High Court in the landmark judgment of **Lalman Shukla v. Gauri Datt** (1913). The Hon'ble Court observed that the fundamental necessity of a valid contract is the knowledge and assent of a proposal in order to convert the concerned proposal into an enforceable agreement. In the present case, none of the criteria discussed are being fulfilled as the plaintiff was unaware and there was an absence of assent about the particular act. This is also an important principle governing general offers in contract law, and a classic example of a general offer is offering a reward by means of an advertisement for finding a lost article. Only the person completing the required task is said to be accepting the offer.

❖ ***Rose and Frank Co v. Crompton and Brother Ltd (1925)***

The House of Lords in the well-known case of Rose and Frank Co v. Crompton and Brother Ltd (1925) highlighted agreements that are enforceable by law. The Court, in this case, held that the very fact that the arrangement between the parties to the case does not constitute a legal contract will not ipso facto preclude the orders and acceptances from constituting legally binding contracts. Therefore, the absence of enforceability of a legal arrangement that is expressed under an agency agreement does not preclude the legal transactions.

❖ ***Harvey v. Facey (1893)***

The difference between an "invitation to offer", and "offer" has been laid down by the Lords of Judicial Committee of the Privy Council on the appeal in the case of Harvey v Facey (1893). While the case surrounded an issue that arose regarding the offer to sell a Bumper Hall Pen, the Privy Council observed that there never existed an agreement between the parties to the case. The Council went further to state that for a contract to be valid, a proposal and an acceptance are needed and to make the contract binding. Further, acceptance of the proposal must be notified to the individual who is proposing because a legally enforceable agreement requires sureness to hold from both the parties to the contract.

❖ ***Ramsgate Victoria Hotel v. Montefiore (1866)***

In the case of Ramsgate Victoria Hotel v. Montefiore (1866), the Court of Exchequer discussed revocation of an offer that resulted due to lapse of time. As the defendant wanted to purchase shares in the plaintiff's hotel, and also went ahead to communicate the offer to the defendant, the plaintiff had accepted the offer after six months of its proposal. By that time the share value had decreased which affected the interest of the defendant to purchase the same. While passing an order in favor of the defendant, the Court drew attention to the fact that the plaintiff had not accepted the offer in spite of being provided with sufficient time to consider. As the offer was accepted after six months, the same can no longer be categorized as valid, and therefore even if the defendant doesn't show interest in buying the shares, he will not be held liable for the same.

❖ ***Felthouse v. Bindley (1862)***

The concept of acceptance was taken up by the Court of Exchequer Chamber, the United Kingdom in the case of Felthouse v. Bindley (1862). While accepting an offer proposed to a party, he or she cannot remain silent. If he or she remains so then the same cannot be presumed to be an acceptance of the proposed offer. The Court of law made it clear that there should be absolute clarity in the communication of the acceptance of an offer so as to proceed towards the formation of a valid contract.

❖ ***Pharmaceutical Society of Great Britain v. Boots Cash Chemist (1953)***

The case of **Pharmaceutical Society of Great Britain v. Boots Cash Chemist** (1953) revolves specifically around the concept of "invitation to offer". The case which appeared before the Courts of Appeal of England and Wales involved the defendant, a pharmaceutical company who introduced a new method of displaying the drugs for the shoppers, which could be used for purchasing drugs, and the plaintiff objecting to the same. The Court of law observed that "goods on a display are an invitation, not an offer" instead, the customers make an offer when they take the medicines to the register with the cashier being under the shopkeeper to accept the offer proposed. The Court reasoned that displaying medicines to the customers will be treated as an "invitation to treat", and not as an "offer".

❖ ***Bhagwandas Kedia v. Girdharilal & Co (1959)***

The Supreme Court of India while deciding the case of Bhagwandas Kedia v. Girdharilal & Co (1959) took into account Sections 2,3, and 4 of the Indian Contract Act, 1872. The Court observed that making an offer at a place that has been accepted elsewhere does not ipso facto form part of the cause of action in a suit for damage, in scenarios for breach of contract. Generally, a contract is the consequence of acceptance of offer and intimation of that acceptance, therefore the intimation must be by the same external manifestation which is recognized by the law, or is sufficient in the eyes of law.

❖ ***Kedarnath v. Gorie Muhammad (1886)***

The Calcutta High Court in a notable case of **Kedarnath Bhattacharji vs Gorie Mahomed** (1886), observed that although the promise made in this case was in relation to a charitable purpose and that the defendant, in this case, had no benefit, the defendant was held responsible for the promise made by him. The Court believed that the defendant will be held liable, as it was noted that in this case people were asked to knowingly subscribe to the purpose for which the money was to be applied or used. Along with this, the people were aware that in the faith of their subscription they had to incur the obligation to pay the contractor for the work. In this case, the law of the applicant was recognized by the Hon'ble High Court as the conclusion of a contract with the contractor was made at the will of the promoter, which was to be perceived as a good consideration according to **Section 2(d)** of the Indian Contract Act, 1872.

- ***Durga Prasad v. Baldeo (1880)***

The two-Judge Bench of Allahabad High Court comprising Justices Pearson, and Oldfield decided on the validity and legitimacy of a contract in the well-known case of **Durga Prasad v. Baldeo** (1880). In this case, the Court referred to the doctrine of rule of law that is inherently related to Section 2(d) of the Indian Contract Act, 1872. Section 2(d) read with **Section 25 o**f the Act of 1872 states that "any agreement without consideration is void". Thus when the legislation itself clears the necessities of a valid agreement, there cannot exist any case which walks against the statutory rules.

- ***Leslie Ltd v. Sheill (1914)***

The English Court of Appeal in the well-known case of **Leslie Ltd v. Sheill** (1914) took into account the issue as to whether the defendants, in the case, are entitled to equitable restitution against a loan provided to a minor or not. Explaining the doctrine of equitable restitution, the Court viewed that, "If an infant obtains property or goods by misrepresenting his age, he can be compelled to restore it so long as the same is traceable in his possession". The Court went further to state that restitution stops whenever the repayment begins, and the principles of equity do not enforce any kind of contractual obligations against a minor.

- ***Mohori Bibee v. DharmodasGhose (1903)***

A bench of Judges Lord Mcnaughton, Lord Davey, Lord Lindley, Sir Ford North, Sir Andrew Scoble, and Sir Andrew Wilson considered the ambit of minor's agreement in the well-known case of Mohori Bibee v. DharmodasGhose (1903). The Privy Council expressly barred any person below the age of eighteen years to enter into a contract, and take major decisions in relation to the same. Thus in the present case where the plaintiff and the defendant had entered into a mortgage deed, the same was held to be void as the mortgage execution was carried out by a minor individual.

- ***Raghava Chariar v. Srinivara (1916)***

The issue in the present case of **Raghava Chariar v. Srinivara (**1916), the issue that appeared before the Madras High Court was whether a mortgage that had been executed in favor of a minor who had also advanced the mortgage money in totality, would be deemed to be enforceable by him or by any other person on his behalf, or not. In comparison to previous observations in the case of Mohori Bibee v. DharmodasGhose (1903) which has provided a restrictive view on the liability of minors in contracts, the present case holds greater significance in the current scenario as it facilitated in providing a divergent scope of safeguarding minors in the contracts.

- ***Donoghue v. Stevenson (1932)***

The doctrine of negligence was laid down unambiguously by the House of Lords in the English case of **Donoghue v. Stevenson** (1932). In the present case, the injuries that were caused to the plaintiff from the defendant's defective products were claimed on the basis of the contract of sale between the parties to the case. While it was the plaintiff's friend who suffered the damage, the plaintiff did not, hence the plaintiff's claim could only be on the grounds of negligence by the defendant. The issue before the Court was whether the defendant owed a duty of care to the plaintiff or not. Applying the "neighbor principle", the Court rules out that the defendant did owe a duty of care to the plaintiff.

❖ *Phillips v. Brooks (1919)*

The issue as to whether a mistake to identify an essential of a contract ipso facto makes the contract void or not came before Judge Horridge of the King's Bench Division in the case of **Phillips v. Brooks** (1919). The Court while ruling out in favor of the defendant observed that the claimant in the case intended to sell the ring to the man in front of him, that is a face-to-face contract, whoever that man turned out to be. No relevant mistake could therefore be scooped out from this case. As the property had passed to the rogue, the claimant in the case was therefore not entitled to recover the ring.

❖ *Dunlop Pneumatic Tyre Co Ltd. v. Selfridge & Co (1915)*

In the case of **Dunlop Pneumatic Tyre Co Ltd. v. Selfridge & Co**(1915), the House of Lords delivered a judgment that accompanied the understanding of the concept of "construction of contract". Dismissing the appeal in the present case, the Court held that as there existed no contract between the plaintiff and the defendant, therefore, the plaintiff, in this case, can no way sue the defendant. Taking a cue on the aspect of privity of contract, the Court observed that only the parties to a contract can sue each other over breach of the contract entered into, and the only exception to this general rule will be in case of a principal-agent relationship where the agent was unnamed by the party under whom he/ she was appointed.

❖ *Hadley v. Baxendale (1854)*

Consequential damage over breach of contract was determined by the English Court in the well-known case of **Hadley v. Baxendale** (1854). When the defendant made an error in carrying out his work which was assigned to him by the plaintiff in his mill, the latter claimed professional negligence on the latter's part. The issue before the Court was whether the claim that was made by the plaintiff was disproportionate to the damages caused or not. Observing that losses can be claimed if it can be reasonably viewed to have been the outcome of the defendant's actions, the Court ruled out that the defendant will not be liable to compensate the plaintiff for his losses on grounds that the plaintiff had not reasonably foreseen the consequences of the delay caused by the defendant.

❖ *Dickinson v. Dodds (1876)*

England's Court of Appeal, in the well-known case of **Dickinson v. Dodds** (1876) took into account whether a defendant who had promised to keep his offer open till a certain day be bound by contractual obligations if he had revoked his promise and sold off his offer to a third party, prior to the specified date? Ruling out that there was no contract that was formed between the parties to the case, the defendant had no obligations to follow before he could revoke his promise. The Court reasoned that although the defendant had made an offer, he did possess the right to revoke the same before the offer was accepted by the plaintiff, hence was not liable for his action.

❖ *Powell v. Lee (1908)*

A well-known case of offer and acceptance was the case of **Powell v. Lee** (1908) which involved the plaintiff filing a suit against the defendant over breach of contract. The question that the King's Division Bench considered was whether a person who acted in an unauthorized capacity, communicated an offer's acceptance? Ruling that for an acceptance to be valid, the same should be communicated, and the same should be carried out by the person offering in an authorized capacity, the Court dismissed the plea of breach of contract between the plaintiff, and the defendant.

❖ *Merritt v. Merritt (1970)*

The Master of the Rolls decision in the case of **Merritt v. Merritt** (1970) plays a significant role in framing the contract law jurisprudence. Although the present case walks in the same line as the case of Balfour v. Balfour (1919), the Court distinguished both these cases on the grounds that the present involves parties who are separated from their marital ties, whereas in the 1919 case, the parties where the couple was married. In the present case, the husband had signed an agreement with his wife of £40 per month in connection to their mortgage house. When the payment was made, the wife claimed the property to be hers. The Court of Appeal held the agreement to be binding in nature as against the decision made in the Balfours' case.

Bibliography

- *P.S. Atiyah, "Consideration: A Restatement" in Essays on Contract (OUP 1986) 195*
- *LL Fuller, "Consideration and Form" (1941) 41 Columbia Law Review 799*
- *F Kessler, "Contracts of Adhesion—Some Thoughts About Freedom of Contract" (1943) 43(5) Columbia Law Review 629*
- *S Gardner, "Trashing with Trollope: A Deconstruction of the Postal Rules in Contract" (1992) 12 Oxford Journal of Legal Studies 170*
- *S Hill, "Flogging a Dead Horse – The Postal Acceptance Rule and Email" (2001) 17 Journal of Contract Law 151*
- *MJ Horwitz, "The historical foundations of modern contract law" (1974) 87(5) Harvard Law Review 917*
- *K Llewellyn, "What Price Contract?. An Essay in Perspective" (1931) 40 Yale Law Journal 741*
- *AT von Mehren, "Civil law analogues to consideration: an exercise in comparative analysis" (1959) 72(4) Harvard Law Review 1009*
- *AWB Simpson, "The Horwitz Thesis and the History of Contracts" (1979) 46(3) The University of Chicago Law Review 533*
- *R Stevens, "The Contracts (Rights of Third Parties) Act 1999" (2004) 120 Law Quarterly Review 292*
- *J Steyn, "Contract Law: Fulfilling the Reasonable Expectations of Honest Men" (1997) 113 Law Quarterly Review 433*
- *H Wehberg, "Pacta Sunt Servanda" (1959) 53(4) The American Journal of International Law 775*
- *Atiyah, P.S. (2000). An Introduction to the Law of Contract. Clarendon.*
- *Beatson, J.; Burrows, A.; Cartwright, J. (2010). Anson's Law of Contract (29 ed.). OUP.*
- *Collins, H. (2003). Contract Law in Context (4 ed.). CUP.*
- *Goode, R.; McKendrick, E. "3—4". Goode on Commercial Law (4 ed.). Penguin. pp. 69–176.*
- *McKendrick, E. (2009). Contract Law (8 ed.). Palgrave.*
- *Peel, E.; Treitel, G.H. (2011). Treated on the Law of Contract (13 ed.). Sweet and Maxwell.*
- *Contractual Performance, Corrective Justice, and Disgorgement for Breach of Contract.*
- *Obligations of the buyer and remedies for the buyer's breach of contract.*
- *General provisions, obligations of the seller, and remedies for breach of contract by the seller.*
- *Remedies for Breach of Contract in the DCFR.*

www.ingramcontent.com/pod-product-compliance
Lightning Source LLC
Chambersburg PA
CBHW040744170726
48282CB00023B/128
9789360128647